CREATURES OF LEGEND

VAMPIRES

by Rebecca Felix

Content Consultant
Michael Delahoyde, PhD
Washington State University

CORE
LIBRARY

Published by ABDO Publishing Company, PO Box 398166, Minneapolis, MN 55439.
Copyright © 2014 by Abdo Consulting Group, Inc. International copyrights reserved
in all countries. No part of this book may be reproduced in any form without written
permission from the publisher. The Core Library™ is a trademark and logo of ABDO
Publishing Company.

Printed in the United States of America,
North Mankato, Minnesota
092013
012014

♲ THIS BOOK CONTAINS AT LEAST 10% RECYCLED MATERIALS.

Editor: Lauren Coss
Series Designer: Becky Daum

Library of Congress Cataloging-in-Publication Data
Felix, Rebecca, 1984-
  Vampires / by Rebecca Felix.
    pages cm. -- (Creatures of legend)
  Includes index.
  ISBN 978-1-62403-154-0
1. Vampires. I. Title.
  GR830.V3F45 2014
  398.21--dc23
                          2013027282

Photo Credits: AP Images, cover, 1, 42; Pictorial Press Ltd/Alamy, 4; Hulton-Deutsch
Collection/Corbis, 7; SuperStock/SuperStock, 10; Shutterstock Images, 13; Hal
Brindley/Shutterstock Images, 14; Thinkstock, 16, 34; Lordprice Collection/Alamy,
18; Stefano Bianchetti/Corbis, 21; Elizabeth Bathory (oil on canvas)/Hungarian
School/Private Collection/The Bridgeman Art Library, 22; Mary Evans Picture
Library/Alamy, 24; Lordprice Collection/Alamy, 26; Everett Collection, 28, 32, 43
(bottom), 45; Red Line Editorial, 31, 40, 43 (top); 20th Century Fox Film Corp/
Everett Collection, 37; Moviestore/Rex/Rex USA, 39

CONTENTS

A NIGHTMARE OF HORROR!

DRACULA

BELA LUGOSI · DAVID MANNERS
HELEN CHANDLER · DWIGHT FRYE
and EDWARD VAN SLOAN

A TOD BROWNING Production

FROM THE FAMOUS PLAY AND NOVEL
BRAM STOKER

CHAPTER ONE

OUT FOR BLOOD

Count Dracula greets his guest, Jonathan Harker. The count is dressed all in black. White hair frames his pale face. His smile is full of sharp teeth. The count grasps the young man's hand in an icy, crushing grip.

Harker is staying in Castle Dracula in the Carpathian Mountains of Transylvania. He soon notices his host's strange behavior. Dracula keeps Harker

In 1931 Universal Studios released a film version of Bram Stoker's popular novel *Dracula*.

Transylvania

Transylvania is a mountainous region of Eastern Europe. Today it is a part of Romania. But Hungary ruled it for much of its history. Transylvania has a long history of superstition. *Dracula* turned Transylvania into a legendary vampire locale. The region and its Castle Dracula have been depicted again and again in vampire fiction. Today they are major tourist attractions for fans of vampires.

awake in the evenings. He says goodnight each dawn. The count's reflection does not appear in mirrors. He can scale walls like a lizard or a spider. Harker soon discovers Dracula feasts on human blood.

Harker barely manages to escape. But Dracula finds his way to Harker's native England. The count begins secretly stalking a woman named Lucy. She is a friend of Harker's fiancée. Dracula visits Lucy night after night. She begins looking pale and weak. Lucy is dead in a matter of weeks. But Lucy's body comes back to life. And she has a craving for blood.

Bram Stoker published Dracula in 1897. It has never been out of print since.

Creating a Legend

Irish author Bram Stoker wrote the novel *Dracula* in 1897. Characteristics of Dracula, his hunters, and his victims are still found in vampire tales. Many believe Stoker's novel is the world's most important piece of vampire fiction of all time. But Stoker never knew his work became so successful. The book did not become popular in his lifetime.

What Is a Vampire?

Dracula is one of the most famous vampire characters of all time. Like most vampires, he is undead. He has been brought back to life. Vampires are immortal in most legends. They have the ability to live forever. Like Dracula, vampires survive on blood—usually human blood.

Stoker's *Dracula* is told from several characters' points of view. In the passage below, Harker discovers the count feeds on humans by drinking their blood:

And then I saw something which filled my very soul with horror. There lay the Count, but looking as if his youth had been half renewed. For the white hair and moustache were changed to dark iron-grey. The cheeks were fuller, and the white skin seemed ruby-red underneath. The mouth was redder than ever, for on the lips were gouts of fresh blood, which trickled from the corners of the mouth and ran down over the chin and neck. Even the deep, burning eyes seemed set amongst swollen flesh, for the lids and pouches underneath were bloated. It seemed as if the whole awful creature were simply gorged with blood. He lay like a filthy leech, exhausted with his repletion.

Source: Bram Stoker. Dracula. *New York: Barnes and Noble Classics, 2003. Print. 58.*

Consider Your Audience

Stoker wrote this passage for an adult audience more than 100 years ago. Think about how you could adapt Stoker's words for a modern audience, such as your neighbors or classmates. Write a blog post giving this same information to the new audience. How is the language you use for the new audience different from the original text?

CHAPTER TWO

FRIGHTENING FEATURES

Many cultures around the world have produced terrifying vampire tales. Each describes vampires a little differently. But like Dracula, all vampires drink blood.

Vampire Characteristics

According to most legends, vampires were once human. Vampires usually look similar to the way they did when they were living. However, a vampire's skin

Vampires exist in many different forms around the world.

Flying Heads and Vampire Watermelons

Vampires around the world can take some very strange forms. A traditional vampire of European literature was shaped like a human. But it had claws on its hands and muck covering its mouth. A Chinese version of a vampire had green fur. An old vampire legend from Malaysia told of a flying vampire head with guts hanging from it. Yugoslavia has vampire watermelons. The vampire fruit growls and moves. But it does not have teeth.

is usually pale and cold. They often have mouths full of sharp teeth with long, pointed fangs. Vampires of English folklore are also said to have red eyes. Vampires do not age in most vampire lore.

Spotting a Vampire

Some vampires may try to pass for human. However, according to many legends, odd behavior can give them away.

Long ago people believed mirrors reflected souls. Evil creatures, such as vampires, did not have souls. Because of this, a vampire's image would not show

In many modern versions of the vampire legend, a vampire is pale with sharp fangs, long fingernails, and red eyes.

up in a mirror. Stoker took this a step further. Dracula does not even have a shadow.

A vampire can also be identified by its breath. Drinking so much blood is said to give a vampire foul breath. Stoker wrote about Dracula's bad breath in his novel.

According to some legends, vampires have the ability to change into bats.

Most vampires live their lives at night. More modern vampire tales claim sunlight kills or weakens vampires. According to many legends, vampires sleep in coffins. In some tales the coffin must be full of soil from the vampire's homeland.

Special Powers

Many vampires can shape-shift. They can change their appearance to become animals, such as rats or bats. Modern author Stephen King wrote of vampires who can even take the form of nonliving things, such as chairs or houses. Other vampires can disappear by becoming dust or mist. In some legends vampires can hypnotize people. They can also see in the dark. Like Dracula, they can climb walls.

Protecting yourself from a vampire is no easy task! Vampires do not die easily. They recover quickly from injury. They are very strong and fast. Cultures around the world, especially in Eastern Europe, believe garlic keeps evil spirits away. Many legends state that vampires cannot stand garlic. Garlic may keep a vampire away, but it won't kill one. In many legends, the best

Drop Some Poppy Seeds!

According to European legends, small seeds can offer big protection against vampires. Some Europeans scattered seeds in graveyards to prevent vampire attacks. They used tiny seeds, such as mustard, linen, carrot, poppy, rice, or oats. According to legend, vampires cannot stop themselves from picking up and counting seeds. The seeds would keep vampires too busy to attack. Some vampire lore states vampires can only pick up one seed each year.

Garlic is one way to keep a vampire away, according to some legends from Eastern Europe.

way to kill a vampire is by driving a wooden stake through its heart.

Creating Vampires

Vampires usually make other vampires. According to legend, being bitten by a vampire turns the victim into a vampire.

Some cultures believe people can be born vampires. In Russian legends being born with a split lower lip is a sign of vampirism. In Romania a baby born with hair on its front or back is said to be a vampire. A person who is born during a new moon may also become a vampire. Other legends claim the seventh son of a seventh son will be born a vampire.

In Christianity it was believed a person who did not have a Christian burial would become a vampire. People who died without being baptized would also become vampires after death. These are just some of the ways a vampire is created. But where did the first vampire come from?

CHAPTER THREE

ANCIENT FOLKLORE

Almost every culture in the world has vampire legends. Historians are not sure which legend is the very first. Many think vampire legends date back to ancient Greece. Greek mythology tells of a woman named Lamia. She had children with the Greek god Zeus. Zeus's wife found out. She took the children from Lamia. This angered Lamia. She traveled the world, killing children and drinking their blood.

Vampire legends have been part of many cultures around the world for thousands of years.

In other ancient legends, the *lamiae* were a type of demon.

Some people think vampire legends first came from ancient India. One example of an Indian vampire was the goddess Kali. She was said to have red eyes, fangs, and four hands. She was covered in blood. She ruled over death and plagues. People sacrificed humans and animals to her.

Vlad the Impaler

Vlad III was born in Transylvania in 1431. He was the son of Vlad II Dracul. *Dracula* means "son of Dracul" in Romanian. Vlad III built Castle Dracula in his family name. Vlad III ruled Walachia on and off during the mid-1400s. Some people believe Stoker's *Dracula* is based on Vlad III.

Real Vampires?

Romania was home to some of the richest vampire stories. But not all Romanian vampire legends were based in fiction.

In the 1400s Vlad III ruled a part of Romania known as Walachia. Vlad III was a violent leader. He tortured

The true story of Romanian ruler Vlad III is often linked to vampire history.

thousands of his enemies. His brutal acts earned him the nickname Vlad the Impaler. According to legend, he ate his victims' corpses. Vlad III was killed in 1476. Many years later people dug up what they thought was his tomb. The tomb was empty. This fed rumors in other cultures that Vlad III was a vampire. However, most Romanians saw Vlad III very differently. They believed he was a hero.

Vlad III wasn't the only person to inspire terror in Eastern Europe. Elizabeth Bathory was a noblewoman

Hungarian noble Elizabeth Bathory is believed to have killed as many as 600 young women.

from Hungary. She lived in the late 1500s and early 1600s. Bathory was extremely violent. She killed many of her young servant girls. Then she drank and bathed in their blood. Bathory felt doing this made her look and feel young. Historians believe she killed between 50 and 600 people during her lifetime.

Vampires and the Plague

Between 1300 and 1700, an epidemic disease known as the plague swept through Europe. People did not understand how disease spread at the time. Vampires were a way to explain sudden deaths. People reacted by digging up corpses. They drove stakes through any corpses suspected of being vampires.

Hysteria!

Vampire hysteria began taking over parts of Europe during the 1700s. This meant many people feared and believed in vampires. By the 1800s the hysteria had spread to New England in the United States.

During times of hysteria, people dug up buried bodies. They often stabbed or burned the dead bodies. The way the dug-up corpses looked added to peoples' fears of vampires. Fingernails appeared to continue growing after death. As a body

People once believed driving a stake through a vampire would kill it. This idea is still a part of many modern vampire legends.

decomposes, its hairline also moves back. This can make it look as if a dead person's hair is still growing. Sometimes corpses' skin can look new. Corpses were sometimes found in different positions than how they were buried.

Modern scientific research has proven that these can all be common effects of a body breaking down.

Skin can shed and look new. Corpses often swell up. This can make them shift.

Corpses were also dug up and stolen during this time period. This was called body snatching. Many people did this to sell bodies to medical institutes for research. Many bodies that had just been buried went missing. People feared corpses were coming to life and escaping their graves.

Plagues became less common in the 1700s. Fewer unexplained deaths happened. Hysteria died down. New medical and scientific advances were

Famous Literary Vampires

The fiction of the 1700s and 1800s reflects the vampire hysteria of that time. In the 1800s vampires were featured in many European poems, short stories, and novels. One famous short story is "The Vampyre," written by British writer John Polidori in 1819. The tale follows a man who dies while traveling. But then he appears to live after death. He attacks young women to drain their blood. Similar stories were written throughout the century. These include a series called Varney the Vampire by an unknown author and Stoker's *Dracula*.

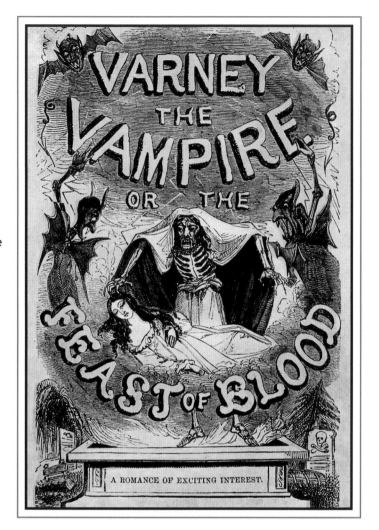

Varney the Vampire was a popular series of novels in the mid-1800s.

made. By 1900 people had discovered disease was responsible for the epidemics.

Science and Disease

In the 1900s scientists began learning more about diseases that humans had suffered from for centuries.

Researchers learned how symptoms of real diseases might have led to the creation of vampire legends. Porphyria is the name for one group of diseases. These diseases can make people sensitive to sunlight. People with the disease sometimes get labeled as vampires.

Anemia is another disease that has long been associated with vampires. Anemia is a medical condition that occurs when people have too few red blood cells. People with anemia get dizzy easily and even faint. They can be weak and pale. These are many of the same symptoms people were said to suffer from after a vampire attack.

Vampirology

Some people devote their lives to studying vampires. These people are known as vampirologists. In the 1980s and 1990s this field of study produced the *Journal of Vampirology*. Today many vampire research organizations and clubs exist worldwide. The largest is the Vampire Empire. It is based in New York City. It has several smaller groups, a library, and its own press.

CHAPTER FOUR

NEW KINDS OF VAMPIRES

Vampire hysteria may have died down by the 1900s. But vampires were as popular as ever. Many early films were made about vampires. One of the most famous vampire movies is the silent German film *Nosferatu*. It came out in 1922. The film's main character is Count Orlok.

Stoker's novel also inspired many films. One that came out in 1931, titled *Dracula*, became especially

Count Orlok of the 1922 film *Nosferatu* is one of the most famous movie vampires ever.

famous. Actor Bela Lugosi played the title role.

The Reluctant Vampire

From 1966 to 1971, a popular television show about a vampire aired in the United States. It was called *Dark Shadows*. The star of the show is a vampire named Barnabas Collins. He lives with a human family. Collins doesn't like being a vampire. He wishes very badly to be human again. *Dark Shadows* created a new vampire image called the reluctant vampire.

In 1976 author Anne Rice published *Interview with the Vampire*. Rice's novel became the most successful vampire work of the late 1900s. Between 1985 and 2003 Rice wrote five more vampire novels. Lestat de Lioncourt was a main character in many of

Dracula the Bunny

The story of Stoker's *Dracula* has been revamped into many modern films and books. Book adaptations include the comedic children's book *Bunnicula*. The book tells the story of a bunny that sucks the life from vegetables.

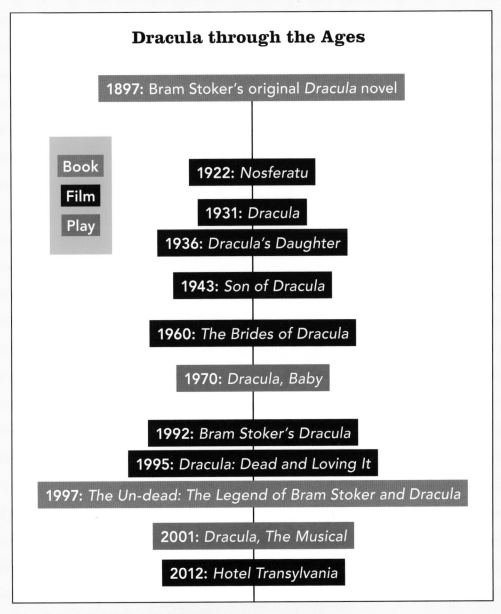

Dracula through the Ages

1897: Bram Stoker's original *Dracula* novel

Book
Film
Play

1922: *Nosferatu*

1931: *Dracula*

1936: *Dracula's Daughter*

1943: *Son of Dracula*

1960: *The Brides of Dracula*

1970: *Dracula, Baby*

1992: *Bram Stoker's Dracula*

1995: *Dracula: Dead and Loving It*

1997: *The Un-dead: The Legend of Bram Stoker and Dracula*

2001: *Dracula, The Musical*

2012: *Hotel Transylvania*

Many Kinds of Dracula

Dracula has inspired hundreds of novels, films, and plays around the world. This timeline shows some of the major *Dracula* adaptations since Stoker's novel was first published. What does this timeline tell you about how the ways stories are told changed over time?

31

In the television series *Dark Shadows*, vampire Barnabas Collins wishes he were human.

the books. Rice's vampires greatly influenced other vampire fiction. Several of Rice's books were adapted into films in following years.

New vampire images were being created in books, films, and television. Vampire legends kept evolving. People's interest in vampires would remain strong in decades to follow.

In 2007 a physics professor and a physics honor student wrote a paper, which was published in the *Skeptical Enquirer*:

> *Let us assume that a vampire need feed only once a month. . . . Now, two things happen when a vampire feeds. The human population decreases by one and the vampire population increases by one. . . . The next month, there are two vampires feeding, thus two humans die and two new vampires are born. . . . This sort of progression is known in mathematics as a geometric progression—more specifically, it is a geometric progression with ratio two, since we multiply by two at each step. . . . In the long run, for humans to survive in this given scenario, our population would have to at least double each month! This is clearly far beyond the human capacity of reproduction. . . . We conclude that vampires cannot exist, since their existence would contradict the existence of human beings.*
>
> Source: Efthimiou, Costas J., and Sohang Gandhi. "Cinema Fiction vs Physics Reality: Ghosts, Vampires and Zombies." The Skeptical Inquirer 31.4 (2007). CSI, n.d. Web. Accessed May 15, 2013.

Back It Up

In the excerpt above, the authors use mathematics to make a point. Write a paragraph describing the point you think they are making. Then list the evidence they use to make that point.

CHAPTER FIVE

MODERN VAMPIRES

Today vampire images are everywhere. Most people are exposed to the idea of vampires very early in life. A vampire known as the Count appears on the educational children's television show *Sesame Street*. Dracula is the star of several cartoons. There are even vampire-themed cereals. Children often dress up as vampires for Halloween.

Vampires are popular Halloween costumes.

The popularity of all things vampire rose in the 1990s and early 2000s.

Vampire Lifestyle

Some people identify themselves as real vampires. Many who do suffer from a mental disorder known as clinical vampirism. This is also called Renfield's disease. Renfield is a character in Stoker's *Dracula*. He is hypnotized by and obsessed with the vampire. People with clinical vampirism drink their own blood or the blood of others. This is dangerous because it can spread diseases. However, not all people who identify themselves as vampires have a disorder. Some people like to act or dress like vampires because they are attracted to the style and culture.

Barnabas, Buffy, and Blade

In the 1990s reluctant vampires were more popular than ever. Barnabas Collins reappeared at this time. A remake of *Dark Shadows* aired on television for one year in 1991. The story also returned as a film in 2012. The movie starred actor Johnny Depp as Collins.

One of the most famous modern characters in vampire legend came on the scene in 1992.

The television show *Buffy the Vampire Slayer* quickly became as popular as the film had been.

Buffy Anne Summers is the main character in the film *Buffy the Vampire Slayer*. She is an average high school student and cheerleader. But Buffy is also a vampire hunter.

A television show based on the film was created in 1997. In the show, Buffy kills vampires with the help of her friends. One of these friends, Angel, is a reluctant vampire. *Buffy the Vampire Slayer* aired until 2003. Angel's character was given his own spinoff

Vegetarian Vampires

Some modern vampires drink things other than human blood. Alternative choices include animal blood and synthetic blood. Some vampires drink synthetic blood because they are reluctant vampires. In some modern stories, vampires drink synthetic blood so they can live out in the open alongside humans. This is a big change from the bloodthirsty monsters of the past.

show, called *Angel*, in 1999. It aired for five years.

Another reluctant vampire was featured in the 1998 film *Blade*. The main character, Blade, is half vampire and half human. He craves blood. But he chooses to survive off of synthetic blood. Blade hunts the creatures, even though he is part vampire himself.

Twilight

In 2005 a work of vampire fiction came out that featured another new type of vampire. Stephenie Meyer wrote the novel *Twilight*. It was for young adult readers and became one of a three-book series. The Twilight Saga was wildly popular.

In the Twilight Saga films, Robert Pattinson, right, plays reluctant vampire Edward, who falls in love with human Bella, played by Kristen Stewart, left.

The Twilight Saga features vampire Edward Cullen and his human love interest, Bella Swan. Edward lives with a family of vampires who drink animal blood. He and his family try to live as regular humans would. Meyer created these vampires to be very humanlike. They are sensitive and thoughtful, and they care for humans. They do not sleep in coffins. The sunlight does not hurt them. Instead it makes their skin sparkle.

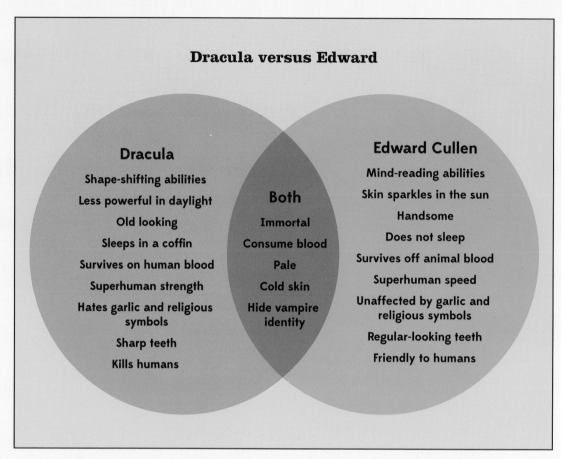

Dracula versus Edward

This diagram compares the traits of two famous vampires: Dracula and Edward Cullen. How does comparing a historic vampire to a modern one show you how the vampire legend changed over time? Are there any traits you would add to this diagram?

Meyer's Twilight novels were turned into films. The films were also hugely successful. The modern, cool vampires of Twilight have made a big impact on vampire legend. Some people feel they are too different from traditional vampires. But their popularity is undeniable.

Vampire legends old and new are not likely to fade away anytime soon. As author Rice believes, "The vampire is never going to go away. There will be more and more revivals."

Count Dracula

Transylvania, Romania

Count Dracula is based on a character created by Irish author Bram Stoker in 1897. Dracula lives in Transylvania in Eastern Europe. He is hundreds of years old and lives off human blood. Dracula looks like a human for the most part, but he has special abilities.

Lamia

Greece

Lamia was first referenced in ancient Greek mythology. According to legend, she travels the world killing children and drinking their blood.

Kali

India

Kali is a vampire god. According to ancient legends, she has red eyes, fangs, and four hands. She is covered in blood. She rules over death and plagues. Today she is said to drink animal blood.

Lestat de Lioncourt

New Orleans, Louisiana

Author Anne Rice created Lioncourt as a main character in her novels. He is hundreds of years old. He is attractive and sophisticated and lives among humans.

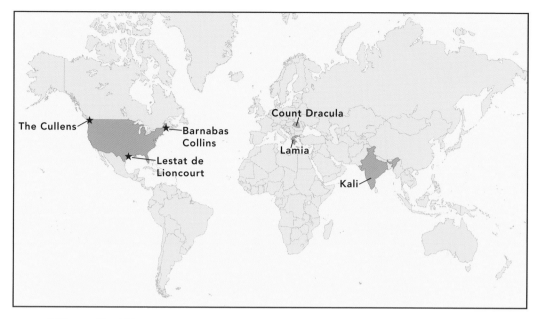

The Cullens

Forks, Washington

Author Stephenie Meyer created vampires in her novels who were more gentle and humanlike than in other depictions. The Cullens drink animal blood and care for humans. Their skin sparkles in the sun.

Barnabas Collins

Maine

Barnabas is a character from the film and television show *Dark Shadows*. He is a reluctant vampire who does not want to hurt humans. He wishes to be human again himself.

Take a Stand

Some people think the modern depictions of vampires are too different from traditional ones. But even traditional depictions varied greatly. Do you think the constant remaking of vampire legends ruins traditional legends? Write a short essay explaining your opinion. Make sure to give reasons for your opinion and facts and details that support those reasons.

You Are There

Imagine that you are being held captive at Castle Dracula. You have seen your captor climb walls. He acts very strange. One day, you discover your captor drinks human blood! What would you do? Write a letter to your family about your experiences. Be sure to include how you felt about each event.

Why Do I Care?

Vampires often related to things people were afraid of, such as disease and death. What monsters are popular in books, television shows, and films today? What fears do you think these monsters might represent?

Dig Deeper

After reading this book, what questions do you still have about vampires? Ask an adult to help you research these questions using reliable sources. Then write down what you learned and a few sentences about how you did your research.

GLOSSARY

brutal
cruel or violent

corpse
a dead body

decompose
to rot and break down

depiction
the way something is
represented

epidemic
a disease that affects a large
group of people

hypnotize
to speak or look at someone
in a way that controls that
person

hysteria
when people get
overwhelmed by fear and
emotion

immortal
something that lives forever
or cannot die

influence
something that affects
something else

lore
traditional stories or beliefs

shape-shift
change form on command

synthetic
a human-made substance
that replaces a real version of
something

LEARN MORE

Books

Hamilton, Sue L. *Vampires*. Edina, MN: ABDO, 2011.

Kelly, Jack, adapt. *Dracula*. By Bram Stoker. Edina, MN: ABDO, 2005.

Stoker, Bram. *Eyewitness Classics: Dracula*. New York: DK Publishing, 1997.

Web Links

To learn more about vampires, visit ABDO Publishing Company online at **www.abdopublishing.com**. Web sites about vampires are featured on our Book Links page. These links are routinely monitored and updated to provide the most current information available.

Visit **www.mycorelibrary.com** for free additional tools for teachers and students.

INDEX

ABOUT THE AUTHOR

Rebecca Felix is a writer and editor from Minnesota. She has worked on dozens of children's books on topics ranging from myths and fairy tales to wind energy and celebrities.